# Contents

Introduction................................................................................2

From lords to landowners.............................................................3

    Part 1..................................................................................3

    Part 2................................................................................12

    Part 3................................................................................19

    Conclusion.........................................................................22

Utility and its marginal counterpart..............................................23

The convergence of profit and the accumulation of capital..............26

The firm, the capitalist and all that..............................................30

History of Economic thinking......................................................33

Warfare of supply and demand....................................................36

The future of possibility.............................................................41

Conclusion................................................................................49

Appendix I................................................................................51

Appendix II...............................................................................53

Appendix III..............................................................................54

# Introduction

It is almost a cliché to proclaim that capitalism is a system of imperfection: from the business cycle, to inequality, to working conditions, perhaps not so much in the west, but just look upon the working place of any major factory in Bangladesh or China. The role capital plays in modern markets and its profit margins compared to other sectors of the economy. So yes it is true that capitalism as a system is flawed. Yet as far as it is goes is capitalism the worst of all economic models. No the creed of socialism in its practical kind is the measurement of human misery. Its feudal ancestor, well the concept of inequality, unfairness, and working conditions that are the cornerstone of critiques of capital would have been a thousand fold in pre-industrial society. Going so far as to claim that those famous socialists Fourier, Saint-Simon, Comte, even Marx, all had an idealised, romanticised view on pre-industrial civilisation.

Yet even with its flaws many have tried to change the shortcomings of industrial society, a goal that was and is commendable. It was these utopians that believed that through the application of technology and machines and science shall deliver man from the evils that beseech him: of hunger, of lacking material, of exhaustion and over work. This was not just some utopian dream conceived by a minority who had their head in the clouds, coming from old money or even from the mind of far left individuals. Even the business men, the captains of industry, especial in the early years of the industrial revolution, many say the efficiency of creation to profit of machines and guided by the idea of the labour theory of value concluded that a day shall come when through the grace of machines shall remove the need for labour while at the same time removing the cost of manufacturing. This was to be their utopia, capitalism and the industrial revolution to be nothing more than a stepping stone, an age of intense misery lifting mankind into a golden age of prosperity, where all our needs are manufactured by factories devoid of labour.

This of course did not come to pass, this utopian dream, to force capitalism to mature by un-natural means of communism that is the great Soviet experiment that griped the majority of 20th century. Does this show that capitalism has won, that in the words of Francis Fukuyama, the end of history, are we now entering an age of the single ideology. Not quite, the rise of radical Islam is one counterpoint, an highly inefficient counterpoint, but a counterpoint none the less. Nor is it wise to assume that capitalism is permanent, after all it still has its imperfections. It is true of human kind that people wish to engage in the pursuit of perfection and it is true of Marx that society has its ends in its own Contradictions.

So from these two statements, is it safe to say that capitalism too shall reach its end point? Why yes it shall, but in what form? It is through this pamphlet that looks at the historic build up to the modern world, and looking at the imperfections of the capitalist system through the work of economics. To try an gage what the next step shall be.

## From lords to landowners

### Part 1

The collapse of central power, whether it was caused by the fall of the Roman Empire or the death of Charlemagne, created flux of civil institutions, social change and the breakdown of old hierarchy's all in all it created a brand new world. The institutions that governed the land and kept the peace dissipated into nothingness, along with the collapse of civil order on a large scale. Which led to the breakdown of communication and with it trade. Countries, provinces and regions became isolated and could only depend on their imminent neighbours for survival, the European world after becoming small, suddenly underwent an imminent growth and once again became quite large. Changers of the macro-level where tremendous, it was the changes in the micro that where the most pronounced. With no central government,

3

regional rulers became much more powerful, a power upon themselves without a central power expecting taxes and in return providing a notion of security. The people came to depend on these lords and warlords for security, and in turn the people where put to work in the fields to grown and cultivate not for the good of the Empire but for their lords and masters and in turn their very survival. And the people toiled for their medieval landowners, till the concept of macro security and governance became such a distant memory that for many it moved into legend. To be placed into service first for security, this quickly turned into loyalty and perhaps slavery to their lords. They became tied to the land, leaving each generation tied to the land to be seen not as humans but as a commodity, men no more they were serfs.

The social structure of the feudal system, while not a homogenous experience can still be summed broadly speaking, up as a strictly hierarchical society, with king or prince as the solo leftovers of centralization, next being the earls, Barons and, lords. They pledge loyalty to the king and in turn the king keeps their loyalty by granting titles of land and serfs to the lords. The lords in turn would pass down their lands to the oldest born son. The loyalties of the lords banner men, where rewarded by being awarded with land from their own lords. And in turn the banner men called Vassals shall rewarded men under their command with land of their own. This created a complex and fractured geo-political reality that was based on loyalties sometimes conflicting, personal relationships including marriages and personal interest. In between the Vassals and the serfs, existed the freemen; men and woman who were not tied down to the land whether by owning it or by being owned by it. Their greatest skill laded in their speciality, they formed guilds, master masons and carpenters, merchants, sculptors and painters. These types of skills had a high learning curve and such became only accessible to those who could afford both the time and equipment. So in most cases, much like the lords the skilled labour became inherited from father to son, and so the guilds became closed off. Lastly the serfs, by far the largest of all classes, comprised by men and woman whose only quality was their quantity. They performed low skilled tests albeit in a lot greater number. Yet their greatest strength lay in their ability to sow and harvest the land. They could in one year in one field plant three types of crops which offer optimal survival for their designated seasons. This allowed for greater surplus of food that that of the Roman times, yet at greater time consumption and labour intensity.

In theory in medieval Europe, the highest of all posts both secular and religious was held by the pope, and granted the kings of Europe the right to rule the terrestrial lands in his name. This created a system where the pope justified the kings right to rule through divine mandate, after all the king all but politically weak and the lords so strong that while god proclaimed them to rule it was the good well of the lords that sustained the position. And in turn the kings and their lands payed taxes to the churches and consolidate the popes' power by building cathedrals. The lords for the most part did pay loyalties to the king, whether it is due to genuine love for their monarch, or fear of gods' wrath, or due to the constant infighting between the nobles, where anyone who breaks away from the pack shall be ripped apart. Regardless of the lords and barons true intentions they would send taxes to the king to keep his lifestyle and men to fight his wars, it was also true that while those around the king paid service to him they were in fact the true power and wealth creators. Therefore if the king wished to keep his influence he would need to keep the pope and other princes in check along with his lords. The lords then would be the most powerful of all the classes (assuming one keeps the king separate from the nobles) and if united they could overthrow the king and rule as an oligarchy. Yet set up in such a way as touched upon before to discourage discontent amongst the rank and file of the nobles. Therefore the lords while in theory where the most powerful of the classes, they were in practice obliged to offer caution in dealing with both king and other lords otherwise at risk to empowering enemies. The lords also needed to take considerable pains in order to please or at least subjugate internal populations otherwise risk a peasant revolt.

The churches role in the Feudal society was simple: to offer hope, hope to the downtrodden to those who suffered the greatest in the Feudal Society. It was the church that offered a simple explanation for life of the serfs; work hard in this life and in the next one you will be rewarded with eternal pleasures of the soul. Heaven regardless of the metaphysical ramifications, the state and by proxy the church used it to its complete advantage in order to pacify the majority, the largest class; it was for all intents and purposes the opiate of the people. For the lords, some of them would have been pious in their beliefs; others would have seen it as a means to power, after all the sons who failed to be born first would have gone into the clergy. On the other hand it would have been universally agreed, whether consciously or not that the church was needed to keep the people in check. It was through this propaganda of hope that made the church wealthy and due to the rules of Europe using the church for its own ends it grew corrupt. From this corruption, grew the seeds of ruin for while the church grew corrupt, the people did not mind for the times where healthy and by some form of twisted logic the corruption was justified. Yet by the eleventh century the black plague had seeped through Europe removing up to around 70% of the population, and by extension the removal of the justification of the corrupt church.

The military much like the government at the time was an entirely localised affair, there was no standing army, nor did the king have any standing army of his own. With no professional army since the Roman Empire and no standing army till after The Hundred Year war, kings had to really off either the good will of the lords to gather men or pay for mercenaries. A costly affair, and a dangerous one, for the enemy could just offer higher salaries to the opposing army, and as many kings found out the hard way, after the fighting mercenaries are out of work and highly trained in the art of war, a dangerous mixture. As many of them end up sacking the lands they once protected.

The end of Feudalism was not an explosive event, the new replacing the old in revolutionary fashion, but rather a more gradual movement that had its roots formed at the birth of feudalism itself. Through the corrosive tools of civil evolution, technological change and environmental changes did Europe gradual change. Now it should be noted that the changes were not universal, along with the notion of feudalism, it was not homogenous, certain states and geographic regions where more economically advanced and some states managed to escape the trappings of the economic state of feudalism and advance to the next state faster than others. Therefore the geo-political-social-economic conditions shall be in constant flux in relation to one another, so in order to make things easier, this chapter shall only focus on the most advanced countries of England and Italy. Firstly to take into account the factors of change as an objective instrument and secondly to look at these two countries [England and Italy respectfully] whose independent variables of why and how they overcame the feudal system.

### Civil evolution

Civil evolution only gradually happened for two reasons. The first being the centralization of power and with it security and the second: being greater freedoms for the lower classes. That is with the gradual rise of stronger kings and the laws of the land eventually fell away from the fractured kingdoms and lands of the lords and towards a more centralized bureaucracy, which eventually saw a universal system of laws, in England and eventually the Anglo-Saxon world this was cemented by the common law whereas on the European continent it came much latter as the Napoleonic code. By having both a strong rule of law and a strong system to enforce this law it allowed a certain degree of security in regards to both trade and contracts.

The second factor being the greater legal protection in regards to the lower classes and while it was only in the 20th century that any real equality was realized. It was also necessary to granting more rights to the feudal so that a potential consumer class could rise and by more and more goods.

The common people (serfs) where tied to the land and the lords ruled over them and in turn the king and the pope ruled over the lords. This image of the hierarchy offered the greatest cliché when discussing the concept of Feudalism. Granted it does paint a picture of truth and needless to say, in terms of economic productivity this state was highly inefficient and because of it created dissatisfaction between lords and their servants and between lords and lords. This usually manifested itself through internal rebellion which for the most part failed. The most successful was the end point of one such rebellion as the signing of the Magna Carter, which granted greater legal rule and greater protection to the commoners at least in name. While the magna carter has of course gathered an air romance around the paper as the act at the time was seen as both a symbolic proclamation by the king, with latter editions having issues that dismantled the monarchs' power edited out. Nor was it an original piece but rather for most parts a word for word re-print of Henry 1st Charter of Liberties. Regardless of the charters goals or originality it has reached a status in the western world up there with the American Bill or Rights or the French Declaration of the rights of man and of the citizen. Quite simply this document represented the legal rights of all freemen, and set up the future legal rights, such as liberty and the right to private property which in turn led to greater economic prosperity.

## Technology

In Europe during the hay-day of the Roman Empire, technologies where prevalent to just about anyone of any class: From the road to the aqueducts to cement. Some of these creations where so well built that they continued to be used right up to the modern age, thou of course after the fall most of the knowledge collected or discovered or invented by the Greeks or the Roman Empire, was the loss of the Library of Alexander or the formula for making cement. While the creation of new technologies in what is now called the Middle Ages was slow going and indeed many of these new technologies lacked any great abstract theory behind them.

Rather most inventions were a product of simple design, in order to fix a practical problem with less that true critical thinking: to advances in warfare and metallurgy. Yet the most critical creation of technology in terms of economic evolution was in the field of agriculture, after all the feudal system was pre-industrial. Such devices included heaver plows that while involved more energy to utilize as it was used not by humans but rather oxen. Yet for its draw backs it created greater field potential, and as this technology become more normalised, it became practical for larger and larger fields to be constructed with lower energy requirements than if it was done by hand.

The revolution in agriculture led to a surplus of food that offered two advantages; the first was that more and more food was not needed for survival but rather more and more of it was going into a surplus that could and did support a larger population. The second advantage was in the surplus itself, for after the increase in population there still lingered a surplus of food which could be traded with neighbours for certain luxuries that this particular state lacked. Therefore a system of trade was created which not only allowed for the greater creation of luxury goods and for the growth of the classes that created them. This new system also allowed for middle men, traders to buy the product of food in a surplus rich environment and sell it off at a profit in surplus rich environments.

9

Environmental Factors

While the advances in agriculture paved the way for greater increases in population and with it a greater class for consumption, it still offered great disadvantages to the lowest of the low: the serfs. As greater levels of population arrive it created a surplus of labour which would drive down the living standards of both the serfs and in turn the specialized classes. Yet this surplus of labour was quickly navigated into a deficit as ships carrying plague rats arrived in the ports of Italy and other ports laying around the Mediterranean Sea. With a rapidity not seen till smallpox would be introduced to the new world , the black death spread all over Europe, killing lords, ladies , kings, bishops and the commoners alike. The mortality rate was so high that the population of Europe decreased and for the first time both the serfs and the pseudo-middleclass (as they, the guilds having grown much larger in times of satiability, and after the plague where much larger than before the both the population boom and the food surplus) could demand higher wages from the lords and thus a primitive form of capitalism was born.

## England

England, unlike the continent, was in a unique position, as it was physically isolated. Thereby making any large scale invasion dependent on both large amount of logistics and planning and large energy requirements, yet it was still in contact with new ideas and concepts. It was this safety of external threats along with the movements of thoughts that created a relatively liberal society compared with the rest of Europe. While external threats where kept to a minimal there were still the gloom of internal peasant rebellion and civil wars, it was the hostile wars such as this that catered to economic decline in England. The war of the roses was both the most prominent and last internal revolt in the English feudal system and ended when one king gave up his kingdom for a horse and another, Henry, Earl of Richmond, afterwards Henry VII laded down the foundations for the end of feudalism in England.

Upon the defeat of Richard the Third and the dynasty of the Tudors safely in power, peace and a systemic unity fell upon England, and as the feudal system in England by this point was already a weakened state due to the three generic changes as discussed above were already in an advanced state. And along with the settlement of peace, minus a few local insurrections, peace as an internal construct was to last till the days of Charlies the first and the Civil war.

The process was best seen through the development of houses; the first true great English manors where built during this period and with a greater focus of aesthetic beauty. Where instead of before defence was the primary concern when building a dwelling, placing greater emphasis on fortification and military potential. This too allowed the greater build-up of the speciality class, as greater and greater need was placed on both the production and consumption of luxury commodities.

## Italy

Italy, unlike England, was not a single entity ruled over by a king and divvied by lords and then subdivided again into Vassals. Italy since the fall of the Roman Empire and the weak foothold Charlemagne held over Italy along with several hundred years of infighting with no viable power arising that by the tenth century, Italy found herself in a unique political situation. With no principle power ruling over the whole of Italy, with the closet coming from the pope located in Rome, but rather a lose set of regional powers, each residing in a city state; Venice, Florence, Forli and Monteriggioni. All in all the region of Italy is reminiscent of the city-states of Ancient Greece, and much like the Greek city states, they were in constant competition with one another for domination. Fighting each other and forming allies with the rest.

Each state was ruled by their own form of political model, either through the rule of a republic (at least in name only, whereas in fact states that called themselves republics where ruled by a couple of noble families) other secular states dropped the pretence of the title republic interlay and called the strongest of the families princes. And as Machiavelli described in the prince not only did the leaders of the states had to contend with external pressures but also that of their own populations in order to stave off revolution. Along with any threats created by the secular governments, they also had to contend with the Catholic Church for power. All this helped to create a system of intense competition that allowed that where any form of advantage developed by one of these city states where utilized to the fullest.

## Part 2

Queen Elizabeth was on the English throne, and minus a few religious and secular skirmishes, internal peace, inherited from her grandfather was the norm, and with it higher level of economic productivity never before seen in the British Isles. While the ability to create was not in short supply, the ability to consume was still in short, leading to a surplus of goods. The new middle class, those responsible for the creation of items of both high time and intellectual intensity where becoming quite rich, yet still in short number and where quickly losing money due to the surplus of production. Through either the efforts of private citizens or the work of the government, they managed to reduce private surplus by placing tariffs on goods that where coming into the country and by trying to limit the domestic surplus by creating barriers of trade. These two policies helped to limit any surplus coming from overseas as for any internal surplus this was solved simply enough. By either creating colonies and move any existing surplus into these undeveloped zones or they would have found underdeveloped societies in terms of economic policy and simply dumped any surplus into the local economy. It was this economic model that created large profits for the merchants, therefore the name Mercantilists to describe this period of history, where a large flux of goods and money took place.

The system had its flaws as pointed out by Hume, Smith, Badian and many more, where there was a great reward in creating supply and external consumption, but was designed in such a way or in the very least had forces outside its control so as to place no emphasis on internal consumption. Thereby in the long run the economy of the mother country became dependent on the good will of the under-developed countries and at home a large majority continued to live in poverty or in the very least lacked the proper wealth to be truly part of the consumer class, toiling away on goods that would then be shipped overseas.

 Looking at two case studies: France and England: they were of similar design in regards to their economic structures, both derived mercantilist policies around the same time, and yet the larger differences were in the field of agriculture. The English Agricultural epoch started under King Henry VIII, a revolution of sorts, where the production of food exploded. Farmers on their lands, upon acquiring more freedoms after the war of the Roses started to experiment with crops, fertilizers and harvesting techniques. Was this revolution only possible in England, perhaps? After all, England had abundance of the three generic devices to end feudalism: (civil evolution, technological advancements and environmental factors). Granted such devices where seen in other countries, Holland for example was highly advanced, yet failed to become the work shop of the world.

To understand the economic and agricultural advantages in the English system is not easy: Max Webber described the English character as that of the Protestant work habit over that of the Catholic style. Voltaire also discussed the English character through the collection of essays titled "Letters on the English" juxtaposing the English political system onto the French, by responding to criticism on the execution of King Charles I, by highlighting the British judicial process with that of the outright murders of Holy Roman Emperor Henry VII and Henry III, which showed the English desire to have a strong rule of law that was at least in theory was applied equally to everyone. Regardless of the reasons for how the peasants gained their freedoms in England, they managed to achieve this freedom and used it to their full advantage.

By the mid eighteenth century, the agricultural revolution started to really take off, as shown by the price of a loaf of bread diminishing in price, allowing less of an English families budget to be used to pay for basic survival. This allowed in turn for greater savings or investments, and over the long run allowed for greater purchases of more luxurious and manufactured goods that where consumed at home. Unlike in France, this lacked both the legal security and economic freedoms that the English peasants enjoyed. These forms of prejudges against the French people eventually accumulated in the French revolution of 1784, which while it created a new political reality it soon failed to secure it by creating economic security, and quickly feel into back into the grasp of monarchy-albeit a more conscious one.

As the largest majority of the English people suddenly found themselves with greater levels of money and with a greater class of consumers, not only was the surplus removed by internal consumption instead of relying off the mechanisms of mercantilism but the people continued to buy these goods that a surplus would have soon fell into a deficit if it wasn't for the arrival of the industrial age. Two inventions by James Hargreaves and Richard Arkwright; who both inverted devices that allowed the spinning of cotton into textiles on an industrial level which allowed for greater levels of production, the age of industrialization had arrived. The problem of internal deficit was solved and the problem of surplus, negligible, the price continued to dive downwards creating a situation where even the lowest of persons in the English isles could afford the most basic of luxuries.

Modifications continued on the steam Engine by such great names as Thomas Newcomer and James Watt allowing for goods to be produced in greater quantity with greater diminishing prices. The guilds, relics from feudalism, where removed and replaced with the creation of more formal positions, specialties: which become more specialised, doctors, lawyers, technicians and factory managers, the essence of the middle class. And started competing with the landed gentry, the original aristocracy, in England this came to a head around 1830s where the two classes started to blur due to intermarriage between the two classes. Unlike in France where the competition between the old money and the new came to a head in a bloody revolution, the middle class, the bourgeoisie killed the king and the aristocracy due to their economic inefficiencies. Yet in England at least the cat was out of the bag and for the first time in its history both demand and supply where in an equilibrium and in high frequency.

The high process of industrialization in England led it becoming the richest nation in the world and as one spectator observed and universal agreed upon that it was the factory of the world, producing so much so that in order to starve off a surplus once again that they initiated the second empire after the American Revolution. India, Canada, Australia, South Africa and many more became part of the English trading block. The process of mass industrialization became so successful that the rest of the world quickly adopted this new economic model. By the 1880s Western Europe, including France and the newly formed German states, along with non-European countries; Japan, which opened up to the west by the American Captain Perry, and the USA where by the 1880s after their civil war and the process to rebuild emerged as the largest economy in terms of GDP.

The sudden emergence of these new markets led to a greater surplus of great minds working on inventing technologies or improving on existing inventions or organizational forms. Leading to what was dubbed the second industrial revolution; electricity, faster communication and transportation, the internal combustion engine, oil/petrol as a fuel source and the last improvements on the steam engine. All these inventions went into the further creation of consumer products and once again the other side of the equation, that being consumption failed to keep up and a surplus once again raised its head.

This surplus was reduced somewhat by the onset of World War I, the last gasp of the age of imperialism, in order to remove existing surplus and create a profit, the great powers rushed off to create greater and greater trading blocs-effectively called colonies-a neo-mercantilism system of sorts.

Naturally Germany only forming after the Franco-Prussian war was late to the game of colonial expansion and as such tension was building till eventual by 1914 hostilities broke out and the Great War began. With victory in the hands of the old colonists, production once again started to fuel the surplus of the consumer with the middle class slowly growing along with GDP. Alas demand could not keep up with production and along with the financial bubble and the long drought of credit plunged the world into the great depression. Demand truly stagged and with it for the first time production. It was the type of environment that fostered all forms of isms from communism and socialism to fascism, all competing for dominance.

It also created the environment that allowed for the creation of the twentieth century's greatest economic theory. John Maynard Keynes and his work "the general theory of Employment, interest and money" which at least in the short run would lead to the removal of the neo-classical model of economics that the markets if labours wages are flexible, shall fix themselves. Keynes on the other hand argued that occasionally markets shall find themselves with so little demand, that the only hope of recovery would be through artificial creation of demand by an outside force-the government. The Keynesian way of thinking was/is very much like a vaccine, where a vaccine places a benign aliment into the body to stave off the full effect, Keynesian polices relished a benign form of socialism into the body [the market] in order to stave off the full aliment in this case communism. And it worked the great economies of the world the USA, England, France and to a lesser extent or perhaps to a greater extent Germany managed to not fall into the cravats of communism.

Eventually world war two broke out, for the European front in 1939 and the Japanese front 1937. The reasons for the German front where divided into two spheres; the first laded in the defeat of Germany in the first world war and the psychological scar it left over the defeat of the nation, the loss of national pride, the loss of economic control, the dismantling of the German military and its projections of its foreign power. The German people where utterly defeated and all it took was the men of the NAZI party along with their leader Adolf Hitler to utilize the frustrations, the lost pride and the fatalism of the German people to put them in power. All the more remarkable as German had the highest percentage of middle class to working class ratio in Europe.

The second was in more economic terms, even though the German economy was effectively stripped down to its most basic components, and even though Germany had the largest consumer class in Europe if not the world they still needed more land, more breathing space more of an economy. As such, German imperialism marched on top of Europe yet again before being put back into its box by a combined force of Russian, English, and American militaries. Japan on the other hand was remarkably different than the European or American powers at the time, rather they before 1854 remained in a state of hostile isolation till Commander Perry opened up Japan to the west. The opening was such a success that by 1867 the Japanese government re-organised itself into a centrally controlled bureaucracy with strong empresses on industrialization.

While Japan was quickly coming to; political, economic, technological, and social change it was hindered by its geographic nature. Due to being a collection of islands and rescores poor its industry was at the mercy of neighbouring countries and their price of raw rescores. Eventually this lack of useful land for Japan evolved into imperial ambition. Firstly by annexing the ocean boarders of China and Korea, the war with Russia in the Russo-Japanese the first time in modern history where a none-European power defeated a great power and further annexation of China. They soon became too big for their boots and threatened Western interests, especial America. Ordering the removal of much needed oil for both the Japanese war machine and their economy, they of course retaliated in the form of Pearl Harbour and with that America became formally involved in the Second World War.

The USA, the last world war was most kind to her, the kindest in fact; after all she survived with her industrial not only still intact but by then a highly precise instrument, the result of greater organisational form and greater technological abilities. The benefits of an economy tuned for war yet none of the negatives of enemy bombs and planes. The USA also arose out of its shyness cum isolationism into the spearhead of communism deterrence that was the cold war. Focusing on the economic developments of the USA, two things need to be minded. The first being that the USA already the predominate powerhouse of the world, underwent major retooling into a singular purpose-to build military hardware. The war also allowed for greater ability of consumption, consumption for military purpose, but consumption none the less. It was this greater equality between supply and demand that allowed for greater research into manufacturing efficiency.

World War II was dubbed the physicist war, the reasons are clear, with the inventions of RADER, computers-to a degree-, the V1 and V2 rockets and of course the nuclear bomb all fuelled this title. This brings up the second point, that the manufacturing arm of the

American economy became highly specialised with more and more jobs depending on higher skilled labour. This bias of labour eventually manifested itself into the form of the returning GIs' heading off to university and eventually too their off spring as the baby boomers. Higher education and specialisation led to the greatest growth of the middle class in history, yet alas, the further perfection of manufacturing led to yet again to further supply surpluses. Yet instead of agreeing to greater movements of imperial pursuit, America and indeed the rest of the Western world tried something entirely radical and new.

When discussing the twentieth century, the most impressive people of the last century include Einstein, Bob Dylan, Winston Churchill, and of course Alfred Fraud. Yet it was Frauds American nephew Edward Bernays who revolutionised the world. Bernays through his work argued that by applying the psychology of mob mentality with that of his uncles' work in psychoanalyse he believed he had created a great good. That in order to control the crowd which he claimed where irrational and dangerous and therefore needed to be controlled by a benevolent government, the means to the ends he argued was through public relations and propaganda. His work was adopted by such programmes such as presidential elections and the German Propaganda machine under the tenure of Gobbles. Yet the biggest contribution was towards marketing, by equating the Freudian sub conscious with that of goods produced. In other words by using sexual tension or any other tension to sell an item they have managed to trick consumers to equate wants with needs. So to recap with the diminishing costs of manufacturing, the rising class of consumers and the equalizing of wants and needs, that by the middle of the twentieth century the danger of the build-up of surplus was finally removed, as long as consumer money was freely around.

## Part 3

As young and not so young people in the western world headed off to higher and higher education and as industries became more and more high tech and specialised, and after World War II most countries in the western world either due to economic circumstances or due to the formation of constitutions granting workers basic rights which were imposed onto the defeated axis powers formed unions. For the first time in modern history the powers that be- that being the government- set precedence by siding with labour over capital. The wages of labour from the western world continued to rise till the mid-seventies in the western world in general and the USA specifically. Due to lack of raw rescores in the form of oil and due to high unemployment and high inflation the Philips curve failed to shape up and wages remained stagnant. By the time of the presidency of Jimmy Carter this new economic reality was in the mindset of becoming a permanent new epoch of capitalism. After all the Keynesian models failed to work, and the economic model remained stagnate. A silent revolution then took hold in the Western World, a rejection of the liberal economic model and with it neo-Keynesian thinking. The rise of Milton Friedman and his theories on monetarism argued that Keynesian policies are redundant as long as the Federal Reserve does its job monitoring the money supply. This rejection of classical macroeconomic theory also led to a revolution in the realm of politics. With most countries in the western world accepting the policies of restraint and austerity as pioneered by the leaders Margret Thatcher in Great Britain and Ronald Reagan in the States, who ushered in a new era less for more.

The first action of the 40th president was to take action against air traffic controllers strike, while the air traffic controllers where violating federal law which prohibit federal unions from striking, in spite of the law the air traffic controllers went on strike and Ronal Reagan gave the strikers 48 hours to terminate the strike or they employment would be terminated. They called the bluff and in turn where fired. The order while on its own was inconsequential, it broke a precedent set by the environment of the great depression that the government favours labour over capital. As one commentator argued it sent a clear message to the private sector that unions need no longer be feared. This was also mirrored by Margret Thatcher in England who hunted down and effectively destroyed the coal mining unions which once again set a signal to capital that they were in favour with the administration at the peril of labour.

The problem was further exuberated by Clinton's free trade acts which freed many industrial bases of not only the problem of unionised labour but also the trappings of one's citizens' altogether. The exodus of industrialisation led to two prominent changes. The first being that with globalization the west became more a service based industry while the east became more an industrial based industry, yet still catering goods to the west. An old paradigm has re-invented itself, globalisation a new face yet the same old social structure, the west posing as the middle class, the east as seen as the proletariat, and the moneyed class, the true capitalists being somewhat uniformly distributed geographically.

The second change is so not much a change as a stagflation of wages. Beginning in the 1970s for whatever reason most likely the blind pursuit of greed, real wages have remained quite stagnant yet the constant growth of consumption by the west tells of some new factor coming into play in the supply and demand models. The new variable was credit easy and cheap credit added with suppler propaganda the swap between needs and wants led to a dangerous mix. An economy built on credit and debt led to one of the greatest economic disasters of all time. The global financial crisis originating in 2007 and brought about by the fact that a large margin of people who were issued out cheap credit failed to repay and bought the system down.

## Conclusion

In essence these three parts-from lords to landowners, is both a very European centric or in the very least a very western-centric perspective on economic growth. Secondly it is in a way a particular take on trade, at least in a very western centric manner. That is trade is in essence not only Ricardo's' model for wealth creation, but also a means to starve off unnecessary wealth destruction in the form of surplus of goods. Looking at it another way, a lack of consumption in country A, whereas a surplus of demand in country B. as to retain a surplus of goods in country A is both economically inefficient and costly, two things the capitalist despises. So in order to retain a profit the capitalist noticing this spike of demand in country B decides to sell off excess surplus of goods.

This notion of international trade can be extrapolated and applied to the micro-scale, the relationship between the producer and the consumer. From this the trade between these two characters is less daunting, the producer for all his technology, with the exception of very little things most goods can be created in surplus. So the question then remains, at least for the producer, is how to remove this surplus of goods that is to increase the numbers of consumers. He or she can go about this a number of ways; to increase wages, to lower prices for goods, or to increase the number of consumers. For the first two they would for the most part be somewhat unpopular from the capitalist viewpoint. Cutting into profits, granted there are certain business models were this does not stand true. Most notable with Henry Ford, who managed to pay his employees one hundred dollars a week, this approach to wages while in the long run profitable for the ford company would be in the most part impractical for any company that did not have a monopoly on the car market.

So what is left? The need to increase the number of consumers without negative repercussions in profits. At first they did this by creating colonies, mainly in Europe, not so much the new world for

22

its size and ability to sustain a population. The age of imperialism, to create goods, which many workers would never be able to afford would then be sent overseas to colonies, to new consumers. Eventually this model of trade was in a way superseded by economic nationalism to have a larger internal consumer class. So now trade had gone from a quasi-international dimension about it, to trade reliant off persuasion of consumers. So from country A to B, to convince person A and B to buy product C, where greater consumer class leads to greater levels of spending, and therefore higher profits for the producers. Eventual the trade model moved away from its nationalism to once again something more international.

So what does this show? History itself, or economic history over a period of time is primary motivated by what I called trade. Or the surplus of supply and the deficit of demand, and the need for an increase in the buying power of the consumer classes. So as both history and technology advances there is to be a greater level of supply. Therefore there needs to be more creative means to remove the excess surplus, to raise the bar of demand.

## Utility and its marginal counterpart

When dealing with utility, it can generally be seen as the willingness of a customer to pay for one good over another. Or put it this way why would I buy good a when I could get good product b instead. Utility asks why would this person prefer product b over a? To answer such a question is somewhat difficult, for the truth of the matter is that utility in essence is measuring desires of consumers. As Alfred Marshal put it:

> Utility is taken to be correlative to Desire or Want. It has been already argued that desires cannot be measured directly, but only indirectly, by the outward phenomena to which they give rise: and that in those cases with which economics is chiefly concerned the measure is found in the

price which a person is willing to pay for the fulfilment or satisfaction of his desire.

An emotional state that is almost impossible to express in empirical data let alone some mathematical construct that allows for future predictions.

Granted some have come close to finding solutions, the indifference curve, cardinal utility and utility functions to the more mathematically dense Von Neumann–Morgenstern work on probabilistic theory on utility. So while utility can work in its own system, when it tries to enter the real world it acts as little more than a metaphor for someone's desires in a commodity centred world.

To move beyond this fact, to impose the element of time, one gets marginal utility. Say that I have a chocolate, eating it. It is great, the euphoria of consumption leads to endorphins released into the mind. Perhaps the notion of fucking is induced virtually by chocolate chemical la ecstasy. Open another bar take another bite, and the sense of enjoyment is dulled, take another one, and another, the mind has become immune. To continue to eat, and the consumption of chocolate has moved from a task in enjoyment to one that is labours, a herculean effort. This is the essence of marginal utility. Yet once again, the work of marginal utility still is nothing more than a metaphor on utility extended over time as shown here:

$$M_U = Utility(S_1) - Utility(S_2)$$

Nothing more than utility over system one and system two, still impossible for any real world calculations or predictions: to be only used in special case of logic.

Perhaps looking at it another way is needed, after all utility is nothing more than how much is the consumer willing to pay for an item or service. So marginal utility is nothing more than how many products a consumer wants before he or she loses value in them. Yet to extend this view from the individual consumer to the consumer market as a whole, the view point from the firm if you will, a new picture emerges. So as the firm sells products, people buy more and more of them in let's say a day, it can be any number but for this instance let's call it a day. So people buy goods from the firm, yet their capacity for these goods shall eventually diminish over time. Yet from an individual perspective while marginal utility can become negative, I find that this is slightly false, for while its value may go down it still needs to retain some value for it to be considered a commodity.

Therefore it can be said that utility/value of a commodity goes down with its accumulation but still never reaching zero. That is the function for marginal utility needs to be one that reaches an asymptote. Retaining value yet for each increment of enjoyment it contains, its value converges at a limit.

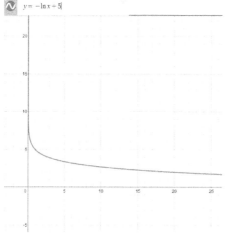

As seen here as $y = -lnx + 5$ where $5$ is in this example an inconsequential variable, a more appropriate equation would be: $y = -lnx + a$, where $a$ shall be discussed in the next chapter.

So we know that:

$5 - \log(x) \to \infty \ as \ x \to 0$, Therefore it is asymptotic, never reaching zero but levelling off through a limit.

# The convergence of profit and the accumulation of capital

When dealing with capitalism, it can be easily summed up and defended as the pursuit of maximum profits. In order to produce a profit, one first needs to creates a commodity, then one needs to gain access to capital and invests it into their venture, which is then put to work buying labour, land and the means of production (equipment). These three devices are then put to work with raw material, man power and organizational form to create a product. This product is then sold into the market where it is sold at a price that either recaptures the cost of production with an added profit, or it is sold at the price that is set by marginal utility. Regardless as long as the product is a success it is sold at a profit. And as such can be represented as a simple equation.

$$C_1 - (L + MP) = p/s$$

Where C is capital invested, L is labour, MP is the means of production, and P/S is a product of service

In order to create a profit one needs to sell their commodity, recuperating the original investment plus creating a profit where that is to be reinvested into the business as further capital.

$$\therefore P_{rofit} = X - (C_1 - (L + MP))$$

Where P is profit and x is the profit margin. To work out prices is simple nothing more than x minus capital and labour:

$$P_{rices} = (X) + (C_1 - (L + MP))$$

In working out x, the last chapter was most adamant about how x needs to be a function that offers an asymptote of $f(x) = lnx - a$, where a is $(C_1 - (L + MP))$so in working out profit in the long run we get the:

$$P_{rofit} = -lnX - (C_1 - (L + MP))$$

In order to maximise profits in the long ran you need to take the profit and invest it in your venture.

$$(P_{rofit} + C_1) - \Delta(L + MP) = \Delta P/S$$

If $P_{rofit} + C_1 = C_2$ then $P_2 = C_2 - \Delta(L + MP) = \Delta p/s$

A more generalised version:

$$P_n + C_{1-n} - \Delta(L + MP) = \Delta P/S$$

And

$$P_{n+1} = C_{n+1} - \Delta(L + MP)$$

To find the total amount of investment over n:

$$\sum_{n=0}^{\infty} P_{n+1} = \sum_{n=0}^{\infty} C_{n+1} - \Delta(L + MP)$$

Seeing if the series converges or diverges: $\Delta(L + MP) = k$

$$= \lim_{n \to \infty} [\int_0^n \sum_{n=0}^{\infty} C_{n+1} - k]$$

$$= k + \int_0^n C_{n+1}$$

$$= [k - c - lnc - C_1 - (L + MP)]_0^n$$

$$= [(\lim_{n \to \infty}] n - \ln(n) - 0)$$

$$= 0 - 0$$

=0 $\therefore$ *it is convergence*

What does this tell us? Capital and its return which cannot reach infinity, due to its convergence nature. Well for starts it tells us that capital has a limit, the rise and declines, the maxima and minima its convergence around infinity. All follow the business cycle, with bulls and bears corresponding with the rise of profits and its eventual decline when it reaches its asymptote. On the other hand from an objective level the business cycle compared with GDP shows something completely different. The transition to a diagonal setup, where the minima of a bear in one year hence shall be higher than the minima of yester year, a system where while there is bull and bear, it is the average that grows.

When those who pedal the idea of the free market as the grace of economic prosperity, what do they really mean? For the more radical on the right, the Laissez-faire, to leave it alone to allow the economic markets complete rein in all matters. Apparently according to them, with no view of history nor of human greed and our predator instincts, this is the ideal state. Moving further along the right left axiom we arrive at centre right-left, better known as bourgeois liberalism, influenced by such thinkers as Maynard Keynes or Hyman Minsky and the instability of markets. Why they can remain free as long as they don't step on too many toes. A guiding principle that for the most part has been somewhat successfully, but why is that?

In understanding capitalism, just look at the firm, in order to continue to grow it needs more capital, and as marginal return on capital and the convergence of profit has shown us, the longer it grows the more capital it needs till eventually its need for capital outgrows the pace at which capital is being invested. Therefore in order for the business to continue to grow it needs to find a new source internal capital. It cuts wages, rises costs on its commodities. In essence the firm drains itself, much like Marx's vampire, in order to sustain itself it needs to mutilate itself.

Under s Laissez-faire system or the very least pseudo-Laissez-faire system this process happens at an exuberant rate, the business cycle, of booms and busts: the panic of 1815, the panic of 1819, the panic of 1837, the panic of 1847, 1857, 1866, the long depression of 1873-1896, 1907, and the great depression of 1929. After the great depression and the World War 2, when bourgeois liberalism took over, the longest economic expansion in history, then the oil crisis and the age of stagflation, the dot boom crush, the 2008 financial crises. This is bourgeois liberalism in an economic stage, not the loss of the boom-bust cycle but rather it's slowed down, and the firm as a parasite on itself, the capital investment this process is slowed down.

So in light of this is the free market system truly the best option, well yes and no. go to any shop, to the mall, notice how the shops, all the goods, from all over the world, almost unlimited in its scope for choice. Compare that with the demand the world over, only a subset of the wealthiest countries can afford such things, their wages being syphoned off to support their only means of work. So it seems that as far as the free market is concerned, supply is king, whereas demand takes position where wages are low but not too low as too create too large a surplus of supply.

Looking at the complete opposite, the Soviet Union, there are no free markets, only one controlled by the state. Was this any more effective than its free market counterpart, once again yes and no. to understand this dictum, just read the old Soviet joke; how do you know if something is out of fashion, why if the shops have it in stock. Now this joke or whatever it is a perfect display of the slowness of a state-run-economic- bureaucracy, men and woman in central command notice a spike in demand for a particular shoe then orders factories that make shoes to make that particular shoe, then distribute it to every shop in the Union. A process that is so slow that when they do become available peoples demands and wants have changed. As for the benefits of the state, simple everyone or just about anyone can afford it, that is demand is universal.

## The firm, the capitalist and all that

It's an almost simplification in the branches of science that there is one model or one single idea, a foundation which the whole field can be built upon. That is a core substance, a subject which relates to all things in that field and all things relate back to this core substance. This is quite easy to spot in the more hard sciences and other fields of endeavour: Mathematics either has the axiom or arithmetic, physics has the force, chemistry the atom or molecule, and biology has the cell or even the organelle. When entering the threshold between the hard objectives and the seductive subjunctives, you come across the twilight zone of the dismal sciences, the anthropologists, the social scientist and the most dismal science of all economics. Now to find the most basic of core substance in economics: I remember when I first started economics, where ever I went I was hounded by lectures and tutorial "leaders" and even the odd parent, that the most basic structure in the entire field of economics is the firm.

Yes the firm, after all, to create a product, the basic necessities of labour, land, and the means of production are required. In order to pay for all this to move the engines of creation is the need for capital, and therefore, it requires a certain Je ne Sais pas, a certain amount of ingenuity to gather the right amount of capital, at the right time to set it to work in the right way, and so the firm and the capitalist where born into a mutual relationship. So it is an almost symbiotic relationship, not quite the Ricardian principles of economics, but an almost word for word replication of the labour theory of value. It is labour that in the end produces the produce, yet it is up to the capital to get the ball rolling. In the most perfect capitalist systems, not only would the fiction between the capital and the labour be not only kept at a minimum, but there would also be high level talks between management and the unions. In practice when these policies are put into place this creates a pseudo-classless society or in the very least a classless society as so far as a capitalist society can be classless, with the distinction between the moneyed class and the labour classes becoming less and less defined.

This principle has been applied to Germany with outstanding results, while on the other hand, England went in the opposite direction and granted more and more power to the capitalist classes, and as of now they are reaping the rewards of high un-employment and a stagnant economy if not a depressed one. Though of course to be honest I would find it highly unlikely that England would throw off its class system in such a brisk manner, after all where would England be without its kings, queens the dull, lazy sometimes brilliant, foppish and eccentric aristocracy, the puritanical middle class and the crass and crude lower class.

While in the middle, the USA has since the great Depression built up a powerful set of unions which managed to create working relationship with the capitalists, who after becoming the most powerful force in America during the gilded age. Found their power fading with the onset of the great depression. So it was with the mutual ground of the bastardization of the labour theory of labour that allowed the greatest expansion in history. Eventually capital once again become self-aware and started to flex its political muscles once more so that by the end of the 20th century Capital had found itself positioned on the nexus of the power hierarchy and labour was at least in the United States in ruins, moving overseas to cheaper lands.

Moving back to the firm there are two truths in regards to the capitalists that needs to be discussed, the first is that the capitalist if he wishes to continue to generate a profit needs to continue to pump more and more capital into his or hers business venture. The second, stems from the first, the capitalists over the long term has a considerable investment in the firm and so it's up to the capitalist to invest time and profit to make sure the firm manages to make maximum profit.

Yet the truth is that only the most human of the capitalists ever meet regulations. The explosion in the fertilizer plant in Waco Texes, where fifteen people died in the blast and a whole town flattened. Yet remained underreported due to the Boston marathon bombings, I suppose the nature of terrorism makes better stories that that of lax economic regulations. And in the same week a firm which produced every type of clothing style from K-mart to the high end stores of fashion collapsed killing about 350 people. These accidents are not new they happen about every couple of years; they started off in the western world, fires and collapses till they moved to the new globalized working people of the world, the third world.

This presents us with a very daunting picture of the capitalist model, the first is the obvious failure of human decency and sympathy, the clothing factory was issued a building warning and yet the manages simply ignored it and told the works to get back to work. The second is the pursuit of profit after all, if the capitalists are willing to surrender the simple privilege of long term profits and security for short term gains, what does that say about the capitalist system as a whole?

If they are willing to let their very firms go into disrepair and to risk any future profits for short term profits, they shall sacrifice the most basic substance of economics to make a quick buck. It seems that greed as and always found a place to rest its head. Its failure has shown that the need for profits over rides even the most basic of long term needs.

# History of Economic thinking

The history of socialism dated back to the days of Plato, upon writing his most famous dialog: The Republic. Ignoring the discussions on metaphysics, epistemology and if any: analogies. Then we arrive at a book dedicated to both the study of normative ethics and applied, along with a hint of philosophy of politics and social optimization. By describing a society that was built upon class; the workers, i.e. builders, craftsmen, and farmers, the warrior class, and the rulers of this society the philosopher kings. And while the existence of classes is obvious they are described in such a way as to move between them is an easy endeavour, based on at least in theory skill instead of inheritance of title or through nepotism. Classes aside the society of Plato's' was designed so as to grant the state, society and the individual as interchangeable. Granted it presents a situation that upon realisation is somewhat a depressing state of affairs for the individual and allows for great abuse by the state and the ruling philosopher king class. The book was regarded as insulting by some most notably Thomas Jefferson who threw it across the room and proclaimed in a letter to his good friend John Adams that:

> Having more leisure there than here for reading, I amused myself with reading seriously Plato's Republic.

Plato's work has been adopted into many different works; most famously perhaps, Christian theology firstly conjured up by Plotinus as neo-pagan mysticism, then adopted into the Christian framework by St Augustine of Hippo and St Aquinas. Yet his work of society was faithfully adopted into the medieval setting by the famed lawyer and patron saint of politicians and lawyers Sir Thomas Moore. was also the first time that the term utopia was used to conjure up a place of a perfect paradise. The setting of Utopia was designed to be nothing more than the juxtaposition of Plato's republican society onto the cusp of medieval society and renaissances Europe. An Island nation simply called utopia and while they practiced slavery, they were so kind to them that one

33

could claim man had no evil. Their society was organised in a similar manner to Plato's republic, and valuables goods such as gold are treated as nothing more than a trivial decoration. Granted any analyses of the work could go either to the realms of promoting socialism or shining a light of satirical proportions onto what Thomas More saw as the failings of society or as a catholic tract.

The beginnings of modern day socialism and indeed the first work to argue socialism as a form of economic model was the famed French philosopher and social critic Rousseau. Who argued in his most famous work The Social Contract, a counter argument to Thomas Hobbes the Leviathan, claiming that the evils of man where not an innate quality that society needs to keep in check but rather the ills of man where derived from society itself. That people where more happy in a natural state and that people are made corrupted by their experience in the artificial construct of privatised land which he called society. With the advent of the industrial revolution, both the great ills and the great positives of society where greatly magnified. It was the ills of society; social injustices, inequality, and poverty. So by the late eighteenth century and nineteenth century and by the works of Turgot, Condorcet, Saint-Simon, Fourier and Comte the great social issues that now occupied the ethical properties of socialism. Following the history of the system of socialism it has managed to gather a following in the spheres of intellectual philosophy, economic, religious, and ethical. It has been found in many forms, in series works of philosophical treaties and dialogs, economic papers and even satire. Yet in every sphere and medium, it has managed to gather a common denominator: that is the most basic evil or ill or inequality is the ownership of private property. From the first man who tagged off his own square of land and proclaimed it his own, to the march of imperialism right up to the modern day, it was the socialists who argued it was the first and original sin.

On the other hand, there is a large amount of thought dedicated to the pursuit of wealth and creating practical theories that incorporate the workings of man's ill nature. The first great philosopher of the modern age to argue such a subject was the English philosopher Thomas Hobbes. Whose work in trying to find justification for the rule of both law and king came to the conclusion that man before the invention of society lived in a state of brevity, being poor, nasty, brutish, and short, and that man's life only improved after the invention of power in order to impose a degree of morality on the people. It was in this model that not only allowed for the use of private property but granted that it was the moral superior to that of commonly owned. Following in the great English tradition of philosophy, John Locke argued to the private ownership of land, but also subscribing to the labour theory of value, arguing that the ones who work on the land are the rightful owners instead of the landed gentry. By the time of Adam Smith and Ricardo, who agreed in part with Johns Locke's labour theory of value, yet argued that the land itself is a form of wealth creation through the power of rent. Arguing that to get the greatest value out of land it needs to be organised in such a way that only a capitalist can achieve. The classical model of microeconomics had managed to move the notion of private property away from a philosophical question to that of a political-economic one. Arguing that much like anything else that was produced the ethical price of land was dependent on how labour intense it was. Eventually through the works of Say, Walras, and accumulating in Marshals work. The neo-classical model of economics argued that the value of produces rests on its utility.

Perhaps the greatest argument for the use of private property was self-preservation, a notion dating back to the ancient Greeks but was only formulised recently: the tragedy of the commons. A paper published in 1968 by the ecologist Gorrett Hordin, in which he described the overuse and eventual devastation of the common land by cattle or as a bigger picture, lack of regulations to the land:

ergo the tragedy of the commons. While the paper at the time attracted a lot of criticism, such as why would the common people be so short sited, as they would refuse to self-regulate?

It could also be argued that the solution to the tragedy of the commons is somewhat of an illusion. An illusion generated by the passage of time. If a private operator buys some land, two things need to be noted. The first that the land by being of the type to be called private lands, it shall be placed under regulation therefore the tragedy of the commons shall be averted. Secondly most who buy private land shall exploit it for a profit. The illusion of time comes into play in that the land owned by private hands shall too turn their profitable land into nothing short of a waste land, albeit in a much more controlled and longer way. In essence the use of private land is nothing short of the monopoly of the tragedy of the commons.

## Warfare of supply and demand

Of course Karl Marx was wrong, in this day and age, it is not a very profound, nor is it an original piece of thinking. Rather dull sediment that stemmed from the death, or a less violent image, the end of history. Where after the victory of the most seductive form of economic and political control that is liberal-capitalism, over other forms of social governing, such as the fall of the Soviet Union. The end of history, the death of Marxism: inspired the coiner of said phrase: Francis Fukuyama. It is as Hegel viewed it, the culmination of a dominate state of governance, which Marx saw as communism, while the West, at the end of 20th century saw it as their own system.

Of course, much like Karl Marx's own prophecies, it seems that the thinking that has dominated the west for so long, perhaps under the mantel: Of we are number one, the liberal-democratic-economic policies, has failed to take hold. Whether it is from radical Islam, even if such threats have been greatly exaggerated, or the rise of china, even if it is using some polices that are borrowed from the west, and Russia, rising as either a new economic power or as an energy power.

So it is true that there are countries that are pious or corrupt enough to resist the call of the siren, and while in some cases, in trying to avoid the call has resulted in a failure of the greatest kind the destruction of the human soul, at the expense of trying to capture some form of pure state. Yet regardless where this form of dissent of the western model is coming from it is there, and as Hegel would have seen it as there is opposition there shall be the anti-thesis, to challenge the thesis and create something new.

Finally this brings me back to what was Marx wrong about: after all as I've said before he has written over ten thousand pages on all manner of subjects: so one just needs to pick and choose to either find truth or mistakes in his thinking. So I wish to put fourth one of Karl Marx's most cherished of ideas: that history is primary motivated by the tension of class war fare. It is as I see it rather a symptom of the disease than the disease itself. For while the economic climate changes, and it being fickle to its ruling classes, the economy shall replace them with a more worthy advocate. See the aristocratic nobles being replaced by the emerging Bourgeoisie and as future socialist leaders would prophesises eventually the economic climate shall grow tired of their leaders and replace them with the proletariat.

As I' am sure most of you would realize that the so called "rulers" of the economic system are in fact slaves to it and when they fail to maximise on their profits are swept away in a sea of irreverence, to be replaced by the next class.

So that now while we have managed to isolate the true motivator of history, that being the economic climate, it is of course the purpose of this chapter to discern the nature of what is the economic climate. Of course it seems that when history is being discussed, in terms of development, we discarded the shining light of the Roman-Greek utopia, as while they were less than perfect by the standards of the enlightenment, they looked like a secular city on the hill. So it seems that history starts not from a pillar of knowledge and greatness, but rather we shall start in the fall greatness and begin the discussion in the dark ages.

 The fall of the Roman Empire, it was unlike the fall of the Roman monarch or its republic: a long and tedious program, one that was not homologues, but rather one that happened in patches and with a fading central power. So it would be seen as individual villages and towns and perhaps the odd city would have noticed that the garrisons of legionnaires would have longer stays of duty, and upon finding their replacements, they would have been smaller in number. As for taxes, well they have found the system for gathering them: that is determining taxes owned, and collecting and transportation  to the Roman treasury, would have gone-from the height of Rome-a highly formal and precious mechanism, to one that not only lacked true cohesion, but also true coercion and so these two mechanisms fuelled each other: lack or deplenishing revenue failed to pay for Rome's armies and so they had to pull out of more and more towns granting them less incentives to pay tax.

So these towns and enclaves of people found themselves with greater and greater freedoms yet lacked security, so it would, the elites of these villages soon found themselves in a unique situation. They granted protection to those who could not defend themselves, they would provide knights, soldiers and other forms of protection and in return the peasants grew crops and feed those whose security they depended on. It was almost a localised version of the Roman Empire and over time the peasants grew a greater

38

loyalty to the new nobles and the notion of central governing became a distant memory.

The economy itself, the feudal economy would have been one of great simplicity. The exchange of capital would have been non-existent, as after all the notion of interest, as described by the Church as a form of sin would have made money exchange seem un-attractive. As for the goods produced themselves, well, a limited number of luxurious goods, the largest form of employment would have been in agriculture.

To sum up the economic climate of European feudalism would have both demand and supply in a limited number, yet it was also true that the two sides would have been equalised. That is both supply and demand would have matched each other and as such there would have been no surplus.

Eventually the feudal system ended, the reasons why shall not be discussed here, beyond the fact that greater centralization, allowed for greater levels of security which in turn allowed for greater levels of trade. This accumulated in greater capital being invested into the creation of commodities, allowed for the development of greater and greater supply. Yet, due to the lack of development of internal demand, there was a build-up of a surplus of goods. Such a build-up resulted in loss of profits for the merchants', they, fearing a loss of their new found status of wealth and privilege placed pressure on the governments to do something about the crisis. Which they did, accumulating in the age of the mercantilist, to reduce internal surplus by placing tariffs on overseas goods and in order to relive stresses at home, removed the remaining surplus to either under-developed economies or started their own colonies and shipped off goods there.

As time went by demand slowly rose till such a point that it over took supply, yet before a new crises could arise, it was averted by the use of steam for mass production and so this deficit in supply eventually broke even with demand. And due to a simple law of economics the more a good is produced the greater the fall in price. So eventually supply over takes demand and once again in order to remove this burden from the businessman, the governments of the world, especially great Britain-scrambled for more and more land, more colonise so as to dump off existing surplus of demand.

Eventual it with the creation of Keynesian themed governments and the unions who in the last half of the 20th century grew in power, managed to argue that there needs to be greater wages. And so greater wages did become a reality and demand increased rapidly and with it the largest economic growth in history.

Sadly, as Lord Acton once said power and greed always finds a head to rest on. So by the 1990s government power moved away from the unions and labour to the businessman and capital and higher wages where sacrificed for higher profits. It almost looked like history was repeating itself again, but no, it seems that the capitalist classes have learned a thing or two about their past mistakes, and knew that their profits rested on the capacity of demand, so they hatched a new plan. One where demand shall be instigated not through higher wages but rather with access to cheap and easy capital, which not only allows more and more profits at little risk to it being damaged by higher wages, but also capital would need to be payed off at a time in the future.

So it seems that the development of economic history and indeed world history is not dependent on class struggle but rather on the struggle to equalize demand with supply. So to conclude what is the future, in terms of this duel mover of history, simple demand needs to come from somewhere, of course the tax payer. It is a system that for those in charge of governments and the highest levels of business do not particular look on too kindly, if it is the GOP in the USA or Cameron's government or the Merkel Government in Germany. But in the end re-distribution of wealth shall be a necessity, if capital wises to survive the coming crises: they shall demand it.


## The future of possibility

The failures of Marxism as an economic model, has of course already been decided by the course of history with the failure of communism as a social experiment. After all the human cost, the purges, mass starvation and the destruction of the individual self by the state, in essence it was the realization of Plato's state. It too failed in terms of goals; it tried to reach its utopian dream, by swimming across an ocean of blood but drowned along the way. In retrospect the failure was obvious, the proletariat vanguard, creating a Rousseau-an society by using Hobbes-ion methods; a short, nasty, and brutish social contract indeed.

 The horrors of state run communism should in no way ever justify the moral or economic frame work of the USSR, and along with the fact that the USSR collapsed the notion of state run or Marxist-Lenin communism died with it. The death of ideology, man entered the age of technocratic bureaucracy, no more where the days of utopian dreams but rather the maximum utility of society and the maxim of whatever works best. Taking into accounts of chapter one the evolution of economic circumstances was not a smooth transition from A to B to C. But in truth a chaotic, uneven movement that in all truth could either evolve into something new or devolve back into some pre-existing model of economics. Its position as an economic model was only cemented when both supply and demand where in a stable environment and the return of profit was uninhibited by external forces. If the economic model is set outside of theses parameters instability occurs and if not quickly fixed revolution occurs and eventually evolution to a new stable economic model.

England over the years was one of the first countries to escape the drudgery of the feudal system and to embrace the virtues and vices of mercantilism. Along with varies civil-wars and political reforms the power of the landed gentry, the aristocracy and the monarch where greatly diminished, in favour of the new blood: the Capitalists. The developments of the legal system and the control of the country's debt by the world's first central bank, which allowed for greater financial stability, and with improvements in the field of agriculture allowed for cheaper and cheaper food stuff, therefore allowing even the most impoverished peasant to work and buy on a full stomach and purse. France on the other hand lacked any of these institutions or developments; rather it was a society that suffered famine in unkind weather, lacked the rule of law. This in turn created a regressive tax system and created an illusion amongst the elites of France. An illusion that the under classes can be taxed at will without any negative consequences for the aristocracy, the illusion also led to the assumption that debt can be flatly ignored. These three factors; famine, regressive taxation, and debt led to the French revolution.

Looking at the revolution in a broader historical context, it was nothing more than the physical reaction of the frustrations of the bourgeoisie and their failure to create a profit at the hands of the last stronghold of a feudal system: the nobility. While the heads of kings and queens came off, and a republic was put in place, the revolution was indeed a failure for the capital model it represented. It wasn't till the fall of King Louie the VXIII and the rise of the second French Republic and the rise of Napoleon the third did France start to take the matters of economics seriously. And for the first time in modern memory France could complete with England in any serious manner in the production of commodities.

The point being made is that the French revolution in its objective place in history was a failure both in terms of its original sprit and its moral or ethical deeds. Yet in spite of itself the rise of capitalism eventually rose to replace the old order. It is also true that communism as a revolutionary device too has failed and yet history shall move on.

The past in no way should be used to validate the future, nor shall the past history of economic revolution and evolution dictate any future outcome. The only light shall be the pursuit of profit and the guidelines of supply and demand: the rest is up to interpretation. And while the next stage in evolution shall not in any likely hood resemble the peculiars of Lenin, or Trotsky, or Moa. Nor too would it come into a stable environment through a bang but rather through bills of congress and acts of parliament, a system that shall come to exist by economic necessity.

The failures of communism besides the blatant contradictions that lies in the makeup of society lade in the economic developments of history. An iteration of every economic system is bought on by the construction of greater and greater supply and the need for more and more demand to balance out supply. Supply and demand the first rule of economic development was bluntly ignored by the perpetrators of the Russian Revolution and so ended in bloodshed. As Machiavelli put it in his most well-known work The Prince:

Like everything in nature whose growth is forced, lack strong roots and ramifications. So they are destroyed in the first bad spell.

The USSR failed as it went against the grain of history, having weak foundations set by the architect of history; instead of a revolution they needed an evolution. Rather the new epoch shall arrive when the surplus of supply is too great and the deficit of demand cannot be ignored, then the new epoch shall arrive and the men and woman of the capital elite shall demand it.

It was the spring of 1968; it had been almost 25 years that Czechoslovakia had fallen under the shadow of Red square. Even though the oppressive regime of good old Joe Steel had ended and dismantled upon his death and "The cult of personality and its

43

consequences" or more commonly, the Secret speech Khrushchev made to the twentieth party congress. Yet even in this more tolerant society, the motherland and her satellite states; political and informative freedoms were only a westward dream. But change was in the air, the recently elected reformist and by then the first security of the communist party of Czechoslovakia, Alexander Dubcek, came into power. A modest man, who if memory serves correctly-and Google correlated- retired, gaining a job in the forestry service in the woodland of Slovakia, after the spring of 1968. His reforms that where to be subjected on to the Czechoslovakian people included de-Stalinization, political liberalization- to invoke a cliché, two sides of the same coin- and more importantly to move the ideal of socialism away from an institutional base to one with greater emphasis on the individual, in other words socialism with a human face.

Alas it was not meant to be, his idea for a new utopia was quickly crushed by the forces of the old utopia, led by none other than the almost mono-browed Leonid Brezhnev, Russian troops storming into Prague, what is now called the Prague spring uprising, which led to the outing of one Alexander Dubcek and the censorship of the Prague media. All in all, the usual disappointment the left of the West reserves for when the secular promise land fails. It would seem that between reforms and genocides, purges to gulags, regicide to cigar smoking, that socialism over the years has given itself a bad name, as an economic system, no an ideological one! And as Ronal Regan once said on socialism or as he called it Leninism-Marxism, they shall end up on the ash heap of history, and it seems in any real sense of the word it has.

Now if I was feeling practically mean, I might asses this development of history by the standards of the Marxist doctrine of the materialistic dialectic to discover the world order at the end of the cold war. Starting off with the pre-existing order of things as shown by the bourgeoisie and her handmaiden capitalism to act as the thesis: as seen as the absolute monarch ruling over the last

44

pseudo-feudal system in Europe: Russia, and a strange inverse of the mercantilist system in Batista's' Cuba. The antithesis on the other as the proletariat uprising, the October Revolution, the June Revolution, Mao's red revolution, socialism, loud and proud, all the workers of the world unite. It took another 60 years-give or take, a couple of years for the trajectory of Chinas political economy to reach some queer hybrid- for the synthesis to well synthesis and out of the ashes of these two fighting ideologies...capitalism arose.

Well that doesn't seem very sporting, the bastardization of Hegel that birthed this broad metaphor of history. Surely it too cannot join the ash heap of history alongside its bastard offspring. No it can't, surely the dialectic is not wrong, perhaps, excusing myself for making such a premature statement, but perhaps the synthesis is still in fact operating. Therefore the question remains, what shall be the new outcome on society, the new outcome on things?

To sum up the economic forum of microeconomics, it can be basically seen as the study of supply and demand and its overlap with Utility. And while by the virtues of the socialist economies in the past all economic dilemmas have been due to supply issues. Whereas in the Capitalist world; depressions, recessions, stagflation and deflation, whether they are caused by either of the two curves, supply and demand, they are generally resolved- assuming one subscribes to the Keynesian model-through simulating demand. To import "artificial" demand into ones capitalist economies, as Keynes argued that eventually crises in capitalism shall become so large that the neo-classical model shall fail and so demand will need to come from a higher power. But it seems, that this form of government spending, this benign socialism has been corrupted to insure greater global financial security for the powers that be. Its origins can be found in two principles.

Its beginnings where found in the aftermath of both the great depression, and World War 2 much like any good drama. It found its roots in the realm of good times. World war one was over and the western world was gripped by the roaring twenties. Then by the glory of the gods, misfortune was thrust upon the land of the mortals. The stock market crushed, sending the western world into its great economic troubles. In the era of foreclosure, breadlines and dustbowls, allowed the perfect intellectual environment for the publication of "The General Theory of Employment, Interest and Money" (by even then) the famed economist John Maynard Keynes. To sum up the dry, long winded tomb, one simply needs to read the 12 page paper "Mr Keynes and the "Classics"; A suggested Interpretation" by J. R. Hicks. To sum up this paper, is easy, two easy steps. One) the market place fails to meet demand, two) it is up to the government to step in and save the day.

The second principle, which found its beginnings in World War 2, or more precisely, the levels of industrial output in the United States during the war. Before the war, there was no doubt that the US was the principle state of manufacturing. But it was during World War II that the US became the arsenal of democracy and as a result created both a stronger industry and a stronger consumer class.

To recap, as of the 1950s there is an intellectual necessity to increase demand, while at the same time, thanks in part to the almost perfected tools of manufacturing that came out of world war 2, there was an overabundance of surplus of supply. In order to resolve this problem, corporate and perhaps some aspects of the US government turned to the great nephew of the famed psychoanalyses Sigmund Freud: Edward Bernays.

There is a certain amount of irony in the fact that while Edward Bernays work in applying his uncles' work on psychoanalyses to that of mob mentality. Which effectively created the modern world; it is Freud who is seen as one of the founding intellectuals of the twentieth century, whereas Edward is rarely known outside of specialized circles. But it is the work of Bernays and his ominous sounding book "Propaganda", and the dull titled "Public Relations" that laded the foundations for the modern techniques of advisement and modern day spin. In influencing everybody from the highest of evil in the NAZI party; Dr Goebbels and Goering to the US presidents at the time, with the election of President Coolidge, yet his biggest influence was in the field of advisement. To equate Frauds theories of sex, with that of advisement, Edward had created a system that tapped into the once thought untappable market of the unconscious. In retrospect it might seem somewhat obvious that sex sells, but at the time it was a mark of genius. To play on peoples darkest fears, if you don't own a particular product, brand, whatever, you will be rejected from more or less sex. Creating a system that sold people, things they do not need, but rather things they-or at least think- they want.

To sum up once again, it seems that now we have an intellectual need for demand, the surplus of supply and as of completing the above paragraph, ability for "artificial" demand to be created outside of so called government expenditure.

In taking a look in simple classical economics we can look at Hume, Smith and finally Ricardo. David Ricardo, born into a large Jewish family eventually became a merchant and stockbroker. So that by the time he turned 37 he become inspired by the wealth of nations started to write down his entire knowledge on wealth creation. This led to the Ricardo equivalence. The Ricardo equivalence goes like this, suppose the government wishes to increase demand, in a region/sector that has fallen into an economic slump, the ruling board of the government agrees to pay a stimulus of one million dollars into the local economy, a certain percentile of that goes to every taxpayer, the more rational, observant and, astute taxpayer might realize that while the government is paying them today, tomorrow they shall be taxed back, with interest no doubt. So this over-cautious taxpayer, instead of investing his new-found wealth into the local economy, decides to save, thereby rendering any promise of government easy of suffering from the economy mute.

While the specifics of this summation of the Lucas mathematical model are general wrong-see that while the government shall tax the taxpayer back, it would be when the economy has picked up again- it is the general idea that I find compelling is ones expectations of the future. When the average consumer looks out towards the future, in regards to whether they should save or invest. It is with respect to the tired cliché of a rainy day; whether it is from their health, to the possibilities of future unemployment, it is these obstructions or negative expectations that diminish any demand, that doesn't rely off citizens effectively being brainwashed to increase demand.

The closing address of the war hero and US President Dwight "Ike" Eisenhower, warned his successor of what he called the industrial-military complex, or military Keynesianism, as a threat to the very heart of the great republic. The complex in question is the triangle of the military using the market place to create weapons at the cost of the government. A vicious cycle, that creates demand, but at the cost of a society with a greater build up for war, a more militant society.

In order to combat this blight I propose a new complex; one built from the three sides of socialism, or in the very least weak socialism, government investment in to education, the poor, the unemployed and the health of one's citizens, to free up their savings into investments into the market-place. Allowing in turn the markets to capitalize off the surplus of demand, a demand created by the actions of welfare implanted by an interventionist leaning government. And the government, who much like under the industrial-military complex, shall pay for it. To coin this new system the socialist-industrial complex, I am positive it shall deliver her citizens and economies away from the tranny of demand and supply and towards a shining new city on the hill. To quote Oscar Wilde, in his economic/philosophical treatise, "The Soul of Man under Socialism": "we shall have true, beautiful, healthy Individualism. Nobody will waste his life in accumulating things, and the symbols for things. One will live. To live is the rarest thing in the world. Most people exist, that is all".

The synthetic I very much hope, as I described above, shall migrated towards this industrial-socialist complex, and out of the battle of the ideologies rose not one out of victory and the other in defeat, but rather the collision of both of them. To borrow the famous term from the deposed Czechoslovakian communist party leader Alexander Dubcek, it shall be capitalism with a socialist face.

## Conclusion

Of course my view on socialism is somewhat complex. Economic development does go in stages and each stage is dependent on the ones before it. A build-up of existing stages till we have reached the final stage. So in history or in the very least European history, economic development happened through: feudal, mercantile, industrial, and post-industrial. And each system managed to advance to the next one through the creation of greater supply and demand. So my argument is thus: as the surplus of demand shrinks and the tools of surplus improve on themselves eventually the economic system as a whole shall be thrown into disarray. After all, it takes capital to invest in the production of supply's, capital which shall be lost if demand becomes lacklustre.

From this one of two things shall happen. Either capital shall need to roll back in its pursuit of profit making, unlikely. Or demand needs to be created from other sources. Now it should be discussed that the human spirit does want the best for itself both present and future and such she or he shall take great pains to provide for his or hers own future. In doing so they shall sacrifice consumption in order to save for a rainy day, as the cliché goes.

Needless to say if such details where dealt with, by creating a new system that removes such economic worries so as to free up more capital for greater consumption in the present day. As such there needs to be greater levels of wealth-distribution, or the pool of consumers vs. the pool of production shall drive further apart and the crises of capitalism shall only become worse.

Of course the complexities lie in the placement of my theories of capitalism. They do not go into the original ideals of capitalism: those pioneered by Saint-Simon, Auguste Comte, and Charles Fourier. A system pioneered not by any scientific or economic principle, but upon surveying the world around them and seeing the pain, the misery and the unfairness about them, tried to strive for a more equal future. And so the notion of utopian socialism was born.

Karl Marx beyond the odd piece of journalism, most of his writings is comprised of being both technical and lacking a certain flare or panache. They are quite boring, having read all 3000 pages of Karl Marx's des Kapital; I couldn't wait to finish it. Yet for all his work on the technical side about ten thousand pages, Karl Marx was and still revelled as the founder of modern socialism. His longevity lies in the nature of his intellectual birthplace. The nature of German philosophy was to construct systems, Kant almost did it, and Hegel was the big one where systems are concerned and Marx following in the intellectual patriotism created or in the very least tried to create a system that incorporated his sense of history-the materialistic dialectic-his belief towards French radicalism and his work on English economics.

The holy-trinity of European intellectual life re-packaged as a system that showed that the power of capitalism was not a permanent revolution but rather shall end in bloodshed and the last and lowest order replacing the second order. It was his genius that argued that the socialist order shall not come about due to passion on anyone's part but rather the mechanisms of the contradictions of society. It was dubbed the era of scientific socialism and to be honest my own ideas on economic development are in many respects quite close to his work.

Yet I do notice differences, for one his concept of socialism much like any before it relies off the evolution of the masses to become revolutionary. While I see it, one needs to use the revolutionary spirit of the masses to become truly evolutionary in society. Yet the greatest criticism came before the grand philosopher of Science Karl Popper and his work the open society and its enemies; that historic convention should not be seen as a universal rule. Granted my theories are slightly universal law inferred by certain circumstance total irreverent to a less advanced economy, but I see a simple truth that shall either end in economic collapse or economic evolution.

## Appendix I

The famed economist Alfred Marshal described the economy as the study of the ordinary business life. Now by all means a perfectly adequate summation, lacking in both prosaic style and a certain flare or passion. It is the blandest of definitions for the most bourgeois of subjects, by god it seems to reek in its conventionality, and I suppose that's where its genius lies and why-at least in economic circles-is still used today.

Yet for all its conventionality I find Marshals quote to be wrong, now do not think this a sign of arrogance-even if it does have a hint of it-no rather Marshals summation is too focused: it lacks any allusions to the transcendental, nor the sublime, it is clear and precise in scope, and therefore lacks the wider picture of what is economics?

In order to reshape the definition of economics, let's take a turn towards the more theoretical and philosophical. So I would like to quote from a passage by the impenetrable Wittgenstein, a thought experiment on morality:

No statement of fact can ever be, or imply, a judgment of absolute value. Suppose one of you were an omniscient person and therefore knew all the movements of all the bodies in the world dead or alive and that you also knew all the states of mind of all human beings that ever lived, and suppose you wrote all you knew in a big book, then this book would contain the whole description of the world; and what I want to say is, that this book would contain nothing that we would call an ethical judgment or anything that would logically imply such a judgment.

So it goes without saying that this big book would contain facts and figures, on scientific endeavours, and cultural and natural phenomenon's. Yet in this big book of facts there is no reference to murder, of theft, or any other failure of morality so, needless to say there is no physical description of morality. It is also clear that while there is no reference to the plight of mortality, most people tend to either be restrained or such matters do not even cross their mind due to their own moral codes. It therefor would not be prudent to assume that this moral code is derived from somewhere.

On the other hand the truth of the matter is that one's moral code can be flexible. Now for a moment to ignore the most heinous of crimes, crimes that for the most part are committed by either intellectual and emotionally stunted people or due to some un-resolved pervasion, or crimes of passion. No, rather, and yes I do know it is a cliché, is it a crime if someone stole food to feed his or hers starving family, or is it a crime for a man to stop another man from stealing his goods and invading his private property, even if such actions result in the death of the would be thief, even if the would-be-thief was only trying to create a life for his family. Now the question remains, who is at fault: is it A) the man protecting his own livelihood, or is it B) the man who has no livelihood but all the responsibility?

So what is the correct answer, who is to blame, or in the very least who has to carry the larger share of blame. To answer that question is simple, it's not A or B, rather a trick question, for while each option has its own portion of moral failing, it is rather option C that offers the greatest levels of moral failings, for it is the economic circumstances that force people into such compromising situations, to abandoned ones moral code for their own preservation and wellbeing.

Back to the quote by Marshal: The study of the ordinary business life. Well he might be correct in that scope, but in terms of the self, the existential, the person, he is extremely lacking. In terms of these things the economy is nothing more that the engine of morality. A term that while not as perfectly adequate at summing up the dismal science, it does offer a greater or perhaps a more holistic approach and so it offers a grander notion of what an economy truly is.  Be economic ones.

## Appendix II

A visual demonstration of the economic development of history starting out with low creation and consumption of goods: The feudal system. On average, only the most basic of goods are created, mostly food stuff, clothing, and shelters, if you were lucky and wealthy enough further specialties would have been opened up to you. Next as the economic and political climate changed and eventually countries that had reached legal and political maturity eventually found themselves with a growing supply of supply but lacking in any strong internal consumption. Next was the industrial revolution and both in very high levels supply and demand. And eventually other countries are catching on and eventually the post-industrial shall have high consumption with medium to low creation.

## Appendix III

When dealing with household costs, they can be readily divided into two areas, incoming capital and outgoing capital. Incoming capital consist of income, and investment, while outgoing capital consists of future expectations, taxation and luxurious.

Future expectations can be divided into two more components, which are imminent expectations, such as: bills, food, etc. While on the other hand risk expectations is the old maxim to save for a rainy day.

Luxurious on the other hand are goods and services that don't fall into necessity or in the very least immanent necessity.

So the total summation of household's expenses would look like:

$household\ costs = \sum x - FE - L - T :$

 Where x is income,

FE is future expectations,

L is luxurious goods, and

T is tax

As far as future expectations are concerned it is as stated above divided into two parts as shown below:

$$FE = (x_1 + x_2 + \cdots + x_n)_{IE} + (y_1 + y_2 + \cdots + y_n)_{RE}$$

Now if the government wishes to increase spending without the risk of mass inflation or debt then, they need to remove risk:

$$\acute{FE}(x_{IE}, y_{RE}) = \frac{\partial FE}{\partial y_{RE}} (x_1 + x_2 + \cdots + x_n)_{IE}$$
$$+ (y_1 + y_2 + \cdots + y_n)_{RE} = x_{IE}$$

Therefore, with the elimination of risk, there shall be less funds going towards future expectations and more going for more hedonistic policies.

$$x_{IE} = \nabla FE$$

Yet with a marginal tax increase, which for all intents and purpose shall not intrude in one's spending capacity in any real way.

So household spending should look like this with the elimination of risk:

$$\sum (x - \nabla FE - \Delta L - T)$$

Printed in Great Britain
by Amazon

41413929R00037